Lilies of the Field

TEXT & PHOTOGRAPHY

BY

YULAN CHANG TONG

Calochortus Books

· WALNUT CREEK CALIFORNIA ·

Lilies of the Field

Yulan Chang Tong

Library of Congress Catalog Card Number: 2001117217

ISBN 0-9710244-0-5

Designed and produced by Rita Ter Sarkissoff, Spring Hill Press,
2525 Daffodil Road, McKinleyville, California 95519
Printed in Korea

Permission to use copyrighted materials are gratefully acknowledged from the following sources:

Biblical quotations are from The New Revised Standard Version of the Bible, © 1989, by the Division of Christian Education of the National Council of the Churches of Christ in the U.S.A., and are used by permission.

Poems *Yount Cross Road* and *Earth Notes* by Virginia K. Anderson are used by her permission.

Poem *April Verse* by Helen Underwood is used by permission of executor of her estate.

The verse of *In The Bulb There Is A Flower* by Natalie Sleeth is used by permission of Hope Publishing Co.

Addresses of copyright holders are listed on page v.

Published in the United States by Calochortus Books, P.O. Box 4173, Walnut Creek, California 94596

Preface

At seventh grade, I was sent to a missionary school. It was a boarding school and we were forced to study the Bible in the morning and in the evening. As many teenagers would react, I rebelled. My study goal was to find what was wrong in the Bible so I could question the teacher. In spite of me, some passages stayed.

Consider the lilies of the field, how they grow; they neither toil nor spin,
yet I tell you, even Solomon in all his glory was not clothed like one of these.
Matthew 6:28-29

This is a collection of California wildflowers. It is not a botanical work: it is a book to show their beauty. How they are truly more magnificent than the glory of Solomon. Some people sing like angels, others praise the Creator with poetry and other art works. Some build monuments and churches. Others preach the gospel and save souls. The only thing I can do is look through the camera. These are the beauties I see and the thoughts that go with them.

To see a World in a Grain of Sand
And a Heaven in a wild flower,
Hold Infinity in the palm of your hand
And Eternity in an hour.
William Blake, 1757-1827

When one gets close to the little flowers, they are breathtaking. Wildflowers are like the love of God, always there. One just has to seek it. When admiring them, think of their Creator.

I will be the first to admit that none of the photos are perfect. None of us are perfect, but each person has some goodness. Like a photographer always trying to take a better picture, we can try to be better persons. With the help of God, we can make progress. Yes, there is sadness and sorrow in this world. There is injustice, violence, illness and other wickedness. Seeing the creation as manifested in wildflowers gives me hope.

The pictures are arranged according to families, with the lilies coming first. The families are not listed alphabetically. Under most pictures, botanical names are given to the best of my knowledge. Please let me know where I made mistakes in identification. Common names are used in the text. There are surely different opinions and usage. We can live with that.

Acknowledgements

Foremost, I would like to thank Lillian Troxell. She introduced me to the desert, taught me about native plants and photography with patience. She is the most easygoing travel companion one can dream of having. We had numerous wonderful trips together chasing wildflowers. When her daughter Dorothy Bradley joined us, there was more fun. The mother and daughter team helped me tremendously in the preparation of the manuscript. They contributed to this book as much as I have. Virginia K. Anderson generously gave me permission to quote her poems and assisted in the preparation of the manuscript. Teresa Donnelly rendered valuable technical help. I could not have done this work without them.

Another teacher to whom I owe much is the late Mary Ellen Schultz. She taught me the joy of finding and photographing and new ways of seeing. To my colleagues at Dow, thank you for watching my slide shows at lunch and giving me encouragement.

Throughout the years, trips organized by the California Native Plant Society, Jepson Herbarium, Dr. Glenn Keator, Save Mount Diablo and Mount Diablo Interpretive Association introduced me to many interesting plants and allowed me to meet many knowledgeable people. These unique opportunities have been a great help to me. Thank you.

Acknowledgements

Permission for the use of items controlled by other copyright owners must be obtained from the respective owners listed below.

Biblical quotations are from the New Revised Standard Version of the Bible, © 1989 by the Division of Christian Education of the National Council of the Churches of Christ in the U.S.A., 475 Riverside drive, New York, NY 10115.

Page 44   Helen Underwood, Trinity Poets, Trinity United Methodist Church, 2362 Bancroft Way, Berkeley, CA 94704

Page 54   Virginia K. Anderson, Trinity Poets, Trinity United Methodist Church, 2362 Bancroft Way, Berkeley, CA 94704

Page 59   Hope Publishing Company, 380 South Main Place, Carol Stream, IL 60188

Page 107   Virginia K. Anderson, Trinity Poets, Trinity United Methodist Church, 2362 Bancroft Way, Berkeley, CA 94704

We have made every effort to trace copyrights on the materials included in this publication. If any copyrighted material has nevertheless been included without permission and due acknowledgment, proper credit will be inserted in future printings after receipt of notice.

Up the mountain and down the valley
Along the coast and in the desert
Everywhere I see the creation
And praise the Creator.

❧ Wonder of Wonders

On a pile of bare rock, a few blades come. They twist, turn, coil and stretch out, making the most interesting patterns. No two are alike. Year after year, I take pictures of the leaves. When the flowers come, they make the most beautiful arrangement. I never tire of looking at them.

Allium falcifolium

3

✍ Dumb Luck

We are so conditioned to think it is better to give than to receive, we find it difficult to accept help and gifts. We have to learn to appreciate and enjoy gifts that are given to us.

This picture was taken before I ever heard of 'selective focus'. We were on our way to Feather Falls and spotted this Fairy Lantern on the roadside. The early morning sun was still low and the flower was under some trees, very dim. I turned the focusing ring until the speed read 1/30 second and shot. I could not remember the F-stop, but it was perfect for this flower. To this day, it is still a favorite of mine.

I've heard of photographers who shoot only when everything is right. I tend to give everything a try, because I may not come this way again. If it turns out well, it is a pleasant surprise. Life is more fun if one takes risks. I have taken many pictures under questionable conditions that turn out well. Maybe it is my dumb luck.

So, give it a try! You may get lucky.

Calochortus albus

Allium unifolium

I will praise thee O Lord,
With my whole heart;
I will show forth
All Thy marvelous work.

Psalms 9:1

6

❧ It is All a Matter of Light

I came upon this flower in a meadow at Trinity Alps and took many pictures of it. The most boring one was from the top down; it looked flat. The one here, with shadow and green blades, looks mysterious and fascinating.

Calochortus nudus

7

Calochortus amabilis

🌿 North from San Francisco Bay, or east at the foothills, this yellow Fairy Lantern delights many people. When placed side by side, it is easy to notice that C. amabilis is shorter compared to C. pulchellus, which is more elongated.

❧ *Mount Diablo Fairy Lantern*

As its name implies, this flower is confined to Mount Diablo State Park and surrounding area. Every spring, it shows up in the canyons and makes its way to the summit gradually, delighting many visitors who look for it.

Calochortus pulchellus

9

Calochortus tiburonensis

❧ Beautiful Grass

Calochortus means beautiful grass in Greek. No one is going to disagree with that. Some of the Calochortus are rather common. One sees them in late May or early June, dancing in the breeze. Some have very limited distribution. The Tiburon Mariposa Lily is found only on the Tiburon Peninsula in San Francisco Bay.

❧ Miracle After the Fire

The spring after the fire at Point Reyes National Seashore, we set out to look for Fire Poppy. We did not find any. What we did see were hillsides full of colors. With the bushes gone, the wildflowers took over everywhere. Blue Dicks, Indian Paintbrush, Sunflowers and Pussy Ears. The Pussy Ears varied from pale pink to dark purple.

We stayed and stayed, could not bring ourselves to leave; and we got caught in the evening rush hour traffic on our way home.

Calochortus tolmiei

13

Calochortus striatus

❧ "I Sing the Almighty Power of God"

There is not a plant or flower below but make Thy glory known.

Isaac Watts, 1674–1748

14

Calochortus uniflorus

Calochortus monophyllus

❧ *Wish I had...*

Regret is a waste of time. Still, we cannot help doing it. There were many times I wished I had taken more pictures of the whole plant.

Sometimes it was because the plant was surrounded by so much other growth, one could not see it. Sometimes it was that my eyes were caught by the flower and did not notice the other parts. What a shame.

Calochortus luteus

Calochortus venustus

❧ *What a Lousy Day*

We signed up for a field trip, but the road was washed out. We went for a hike at Mitchell Canyon in Mount Diablo State Park and it started to rain. So we turned back. The rain stopped before we reached the parking lot. We decided to take a side trail and saw nothing but wild oats. Giving up, we took a short cut and noticed colors among the oats: a patch of Mariposa Tulips! Every one of them had different shades of colors, different markings. What a pleasant surprise!

Calcochortus venustus

Dichelostemma capitatum

❧ Two Faces

How many people see the two pictures on the opposite page and recognize them as the same flower? Yes, they are. The left one had the sun in front of me, back lit, and the right one had the sun behind me, front lit. We often hear that there are two sides of things. The two sides can be very different. Actually there can be more than two sides. The flower may have yet another look with side lighting.

ONE WHO DOES NOT FOLLOW RULES

Blue Dick has a head of flowers in an umbel, usually. So I did a double take when I saw this. It was not regular, but it had character!

Dichelostemma capitatum

Disporum smitbii

❧ *Lesson One*

A single flower makes a great picture; three or more are fine. Two flowers are hard to handle, and I usually avoid them. Here I could not get away from twins. Before taking a picture, I may do some 'housekeeping' like the removal of dry grass blades. As a rule of good stewardship, I will not pinch away the second flower, because it may become a seed for the future.

Erythronium californicum

❧ At the Moment

There are flowers I see over and over. There are flowers I saw only once. The only time I saw California Fawn Lily in its natural abode, it was surrounded by Poison Oak. It had already passed its prime, but I wanted a picture. Carefully, I made my way to it; but not carefully enough. I suffered an itching hand for a week.

There is no definite planning to see wildflowers. They come and go on their own schedule. It is a joy finding them and a good picture is a bonus.

As Jane Austen (1775–1817) said: "Why not seize the pleasure at once? How often is happiness destroyed by preparation, foolish preparation!"

23

Fritillaria affinis

⚘ *Beauty in Different Shades*

The Checker Lily I saw on San Bruno Mountain was dark chocolate; the one on the summit of Mount Diablo was almost yellow. I have seen all the colors in between. How fascinating.

24

Let all things their creator bless
And worship God in humbleness.

St. Francis of Assisi

Fritillaria affinis

25

Fritillaria agrestis

❧ You Don't See It? Try Again!

A friend gave us detailed directions to Contra Loma Regional Park to see this beautiful and rare lily, Stinkbells. We found the trail head; we saw the water trough and the reservoir. Everything confirmed we were in the right place, but no flower! Up and down, left and right, back and forth, nothing but grass. Finally, the friend came and pointed the flowers out to us. They blended in so well in the grass we had trouble spotting them. After thirty minutes of counting, we finally learned to spot them! How often do we see but not notice things in our life? How often do we miss the beauty in another person because we do not try hard enough?

26

Fritillaria purdyi

Fritillaria liliacea

❧ So Unfair

Some flowers drive me crazy. No matter how hard, or how many times I try, the pictures just do not turn out well. But there are flowers that are just wonderful; you can do no wrong. No matter what you do, the pictures are just lovely. In addition, this has a nice fragrance. What more can you want?

Fritillaria liliacea

29

Fritillaria pluriflora

Bear Valley

✿ You Can't Have Everything

On an April field trip to Bear Valley, we saw fields of flowers, blue Lupine, white zigadenus and fields of mixed colors. We were too late to see the Adobe-Lily. The next March, we went back to the same place and found the Adobe-Lily in bloom, but not much of anything else.

Lilium pardalinum

⚘ Patience or The Lack of It

Sitting on a log, I waited patiently for the butterfly to come back to the Tiger Lily so I could take its picture. I was told that butterflies and bees often return to the same flower. Later that evening, a friend told me he was watching me wait for the butterfly and learned his lesson of patience.

The truth is I am rather impatient. I became patient only because I wanted the picture badly.

I come to the garden alone, while the dew is still on the roses. And the voice I hear, falling on my ear, the Son of God discloses. And He walks with me. And He talks with me. And He tells me I am His own. And the joy we share as we tarry there, none other has ever known.

C. Austin Miles

Lilium kelleyanum

33

Nolina parryi

⊱ Take Your Pick

Living in California, one takes the blue sky for granted. Once in a while, I miss watching the clouds. As a little girl, I used to make up stories according to the changing of forms. On the other hand, when one is out in the open, one watches the gathering of storm clouds with anxiety. I think this picture is better with the clouds than with a blue sky.

Zigadenus fremontii

❧ Why?

Death Camas, their bulbs are toxic. On the other hand, other lily bulbs are edible. Why is that so? Why can't I look at the plant and know which is which?

35

Trillium chloropetalum

❧ You Can't Miss It

When someone gives me directions with the comment "you can't miss it" I usually do. Once you see a Trillium, however, you can't miss it. Really.

Trillium chloropetalum

Triteleia laxa

❧ *This or That*

Is it a Triteleia or a Brodiaea? It puzzled me for years. In a sense, it does not matter. A beautiful flower by any name is still a beautiful flower. But curiosity and frustration were eating me. Finally, I worked up the courage and asked and I learned. Not that it makes much difference except for the labels on the slides.

Triteleia laxa

Triteleia lilacina

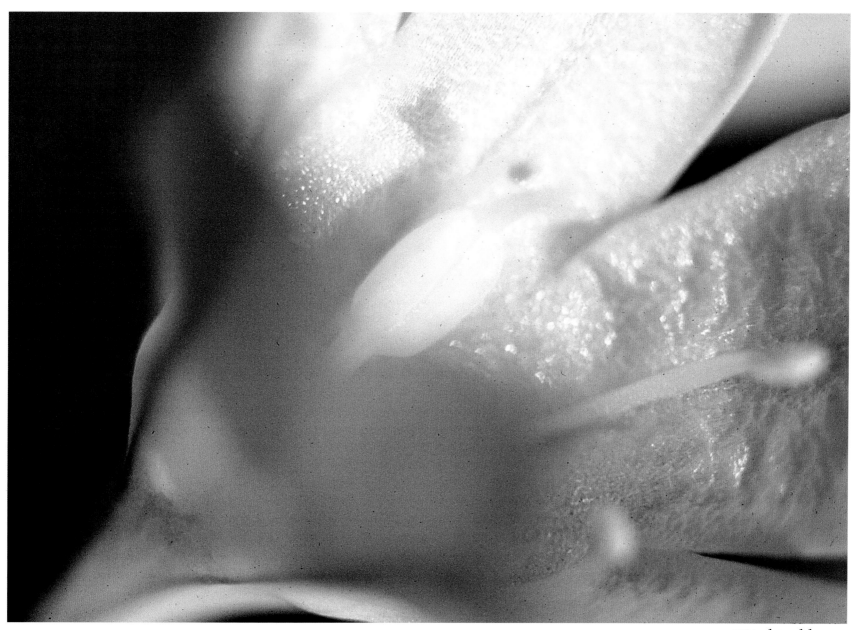

Triteleia lilacina

Veratrum californicum

❧ Beauty Is Where You See It

The flowers of the Corn Lily are heavy and waxy. They look like plastic flowers. I have not learned to like them. The leaves are a different story. I have spent hours playing with them. The way their tips curve, the pattern when light comes through, the arrangement when they line up... they are fascinating. Oh, yes, they like swampy places. Try to keep your feet dry if you can.

Veratrum californicum

❧ *April Verse*

Blue sky of spring
White clouds on the wing,
Fruit trees blossoming,
Songbirds nesting:
　　How ancient a story.
Small seeds stirring,
Warm rains coming,
To give us a flurry.
As the sweet earth is yielding
　　Again its green glory.

Helen Underwood
Times and Seasons © 1985

✣ For No Reason

This picture was taken at Pepperwood Preserve of California Academy of Sciences. The vernal pool, formed during the rainy season, dries gradually as the season progresses, leaving rings of plants as the soil dries.

I like the picture for no reason that I can explain. I just like it, and that is enough for me.

For everything there is a season, and a time for every matter
  Under the heaven:
a time to be born, and a time to die;

a time to plant and a time to pluck up what is planted;

a time to kill, and a time to heal;

a time to break down, and a time to build up;

a time to weep, and a time to laugh;

a time to mourn, and a time to dance;

a time to throw away stones, and a time to gather stones together;

a time to embrace, and a time to refrain from embracing;

a time to seek, and a time to lose;

a time to keep, and a time to throw away;

a time to tear, and a time to sew;

a time to keep silence, and a time to speak;

a time to love, and a time to hate;

a time for war, and a time for peace.

Ecclesiastes 3:1~8

❧ Right Place At The Right Time

One midmorning, I was wandering among some Madrones and saw sunlight on a small branch in a relatively dark area. I took pictures while the light changed and disappeared.

Arbutus menziesii

Arbutus menziesii

❧ Surprise

It was a long time after I knew the Madrone before I saw the flowers. With the size of the tree and its leaves, I expected large flowers like Magnolia. The sprays of tiny flowers surprised me. I was not thinking. After all, it belongs to the heath family, and many of them have small flowers.

❧ *I Was Kept Waiting*

We were gathered to leave, but a few stragglers kept us waiting. Standing impatiently, I noticed the peeling barks and started to take pictures.

To be honest, I hate being kept waiting. This was one time worth the wait.

Arbutus menziesii

Gaultheria shallon

❧ A Prayer
Inspired by Psalm 27

"One thing I ask of God, this I seek; to dwell in the house of our God all the days of my life. That I may see beauty in every leaf and rock. And feel the breath of God in every breeze."

Author unknown

50

Vaccinium ovatum

❧ Together

Not very often do I see flowers and fruits together. I find the combination very charming.

Rhododendron occidentale

ꙮ *Mother Nature's Garden*

The azalea has been developed for gardens and is very common. Seeing it in the wild among other trees gives me a different sensation, an excitement not found in gardens.

Rhododendron occidentale

❧ Yount Cross Road

Grape stumps
rain-darkened, gaunt
stand with limbs akimbo
in wild mustard's yellow blossoms
knee-deep.

Virginia K. Anderson
Times and Seasons © 1985

Field Mustard in Sonoma

Brassica rapa

❧ A Problem! What Problem?

Our laboratories were built in an old walnut orchard. There were approximately 20 acres between the buildings and the road where walnut trees still stood.

Every spring, mustard turned the field bright yellow and we waited for the spectacular show with anticipation and pleasure. Our groundkeeper, bless him, always waited for seeds to mature before he plowed them under.

One year, a manager from headquarters advised us that we should plow the field early, before the seeds set, then we would not have the problem next year.

After a shocking silence, someone explained to him that we loved our "problem".

Ribes speciosum

☙ The Homestead

The people moved away, and the house crumbled. Upon careful exploration, one can find the foundation of the old homestead by the creek. The bush of Fuchsia-Flowered Gooseberry blooms year after year, long after the people who transplanted it are gone. Hikers passing by admired the beautiful flowers. A few wondered what it was doing here, out of its normal range.

❧ *All the Time*

"When is the best time to go hiking?" people ask me. "Any time," I say. The changing of the seasons is wonderful, and I have seen wildflowers in bloom every month of the year in California.

Ribes menziesii

Asclepias californica

❧ *Look! A Worm!*

How often does one deliberately look for a flower with a worm in it? In a milkweed, we look for the Monarch Butterfly larva in the spring, and a butterfly in late summer.

Asclepias fascicularis

❧ In the bulb there is a flower; in the seed, an apple tree; in cocoons, a hidden promise: butterflies will soon be free! In the cold and snow of winter, there's a spring that waits to be, unrevealed until its season, something God alone can see.

Natalie Sleeth

59

Asclepias speciosa

➤ Roadside Weed

Milkweeds have a big umbel of flowers, of which I have trouble getting a good picture. The milkweed seeds are always graceful, like dancers, catching the sunlight in the slightest breeze. They are fun to watch. In October of 1997, we went to Yosemite National Park to see the fall color. One very bright tree by the chapel in Yosemite Valley especially caught my eye the first day we saw it. Next morning, it was in the shadow and the color disappeared. We came back at noon and the brilliant color reappeared. By the roadside the milkweed seedpod was sending out its seeds. How lucky!

Acer macrophyllum

Oenothera deltoides

Oenothera deltoides

❧ *Where Can I Put My Feet Down?*

Evening Primrose starts to open in late afternoon and fades next morning when the sun gets high. A stroll in the evening found the desert covered with delicate flowers.

ꝏ Desert Sunset

On our trip to Joshua Tree National Monument, Lillian wanted a picture of one particular Joshua Tree. We stopped by the side of the road and I saw the desert floor of Evening Primroses and grasses, colors enriched by the setting sun.

Some people call it Farewell-to-Spring, others call it Herald-of-Summer. In late spring or early summer, this lovely little flower appears everywhere.

Clarkia gracilis

Sisyrinchium bellum

❧ Beautiful Weed

Early in the morning, on the way out, there is nothing but weedy grass. Come noon, all the Blue-Eye-Grass open to make beautiful patches. The delicate blue veins on blue petals and the bright yellow center make one slow down and admire.

In the morning it flourishes and
  is renewed;
  in the evening it fades and withers.
So teach us to count our days
  that we may gain a wise heart.
Satisfy us in the morning
  with your steadfast love,
so that we may rejoice
  and be glad all our days.

Psalm 90: 6, 12, 14

Sisyrinchium bellum

67

Iris douglasiana

68

Iris douglasiana

❧ Finally, I Understand

A painter friend tried to teach me to enjoy abstract paintings and I did not get it. Not until I started taking close-up pictures and saw that lines, forms, and colors made beautiful pictures.

69

Iris douglasiana

But this I call to mind,
and therefore I have hope:
The steadfast love of the Lord never ceases,
his mercies never come to an end;
They are new every morning;
great is your faithfulness.

Lamentations 3:21-23

Delphinium parryi

72

☙ Rules and Exceptions

After my first English class in seventh grade, I told my sister I did not like English. Not only were there rules, there were also exceptions to the rules, much too complicated.

Usually, I find it easier to remember common names than botanical names. Delphinium is the exception. The spur resembles a dolphin, thus Delphinium. It is much easier to remember than Larkspur.

Delphinium nudicaule

73

Aquilegia formosa

74

❧ Unwrapping

I remember watching a time-lapse movie of a flower opening; I was in awe of its beauty.

When a bud opens to a flower, it goes through different stages. The Columbine is the most dramatic of all. In the beginning, it looks like a heart, then it looks like a lantern, and eventually it looks like a bird ready to take flight.

When I come to a meadow with Columbine flowers dancing all around me, my spirit soars also.

Eremalche rotundifolia

ᴥ Do You Believe Me?

This fun mallow has five petals and each petal has a red spot. It was most aptly named Desert-Five-Spot. Hard as I tried, I could not show all five spots unless I forced the petals flat. I did not want to crush the flower, so you just have to take my word for it.

76

❧ Slow Down

There were a couple of bushes about ten feet tall by the roadside. Each spring, the bushes were covered with pink mallows. That was the benefit of a winding road. One had to slow down and see more along the way.

Malacothamnus fasciculatus

77

Sidalcea malviflora

78

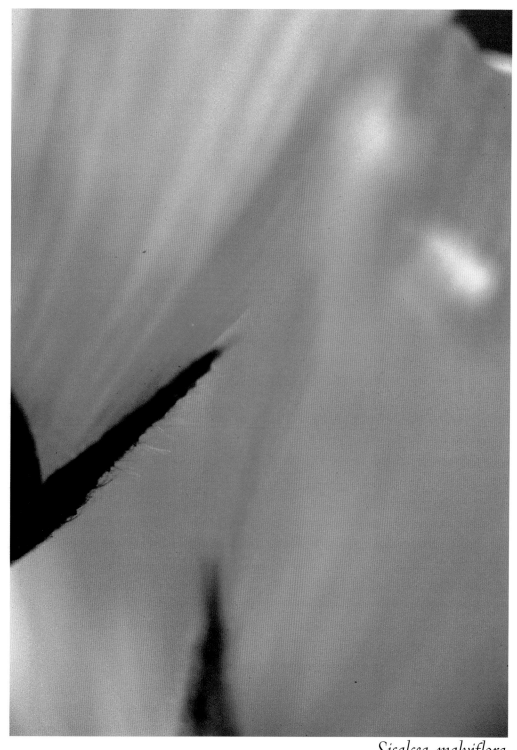

Sisalcea malviflora

Leptodactylon californicum

Linanthus parryea

❧ Contrast

The wheeling pink dancers on the opposite page *vs.* the sedate white meditator on this page. The sand, the shadow and solitude give the picture a tranquility I like.

Claytonia gypsophiloides

What a Sight

Turn a corner, a pink carpet with thousands of little flowers greets you.
What could be better?

🌿 Miner's Lettuce

The name conjures up a romantic picture of Forty-niners laboring at the mines without a vegetable garden and having to gather this round disc of green from the field for food. I never have enough courage to try it.

Claytonia perfoliata

Lewisia rediviva

❧ *It Was Hard To Believe*

In spring, rosettes of little green tubes show up on the rock. I waited to see the tiny flowers that would be coming. Instead, large, exquisite white flowers came. So much for prediction!

84

Lewisia rediviva

All things bright and beautiful,
All creatures great and small,
All things wise and wonderful:
The Lord God made them all.

Each little flower that opens,
Each little bird that sings,
He made their glowing colors,
He made their tiny wings.

Cecil Frances Alexander, 1818–1895

Black Diamond Mine Regional Park

It took us four hours to walk the one-mile Loop Trail at Black Diamond Mine Regional Park. There were so many flowers to see. We became tired, hungry and thirsty, and were ready to call it a day. Then we turned the corner and saw the hillside white with dancing Shooting Stars. Our energy miraculously reappeared. Cameras were reloaded and we had a ball.

Dodecatheon clevelandii

Dodecatheon hendersonii

87

Senecio greenei

❧ A Good Teacher Is A Treasure

I wish the picture were better, to do him justice. I have to tell the story.

After the June 1994 Jepson Symposium, I was fortunate to be in a workshop led by the late Prof. Stebbins. We covered the section of area between the central-north coast and the great valley and saw many exciting plants. Senecio greenei was one of them at the end of the two-day trip. Dr. Stebbins was very concerned that we saw it. He was in his eighties and walked slowly with a cane. When he talked about plants, his eyes sparkled and the love he held for plants reached out to all around him. One could not help but become a plant lover. What a great teacher!

Helianthella castanea

❧ Up or Down

After a six-week course on the sunflower family, I was resigned to the conclusion; I would never be able to identify them. However, it does not mean I will not take their pictures. This picture of Mount Diablo Sunflower can be looked at with the insect going up or down. Most likely the flower faced up, so the insect was neither going up nor down.

Cornus sessilis

❧ Things I Miss

First rule of gardening: Don't fight Mother Nature. For years I tried to grow lilac in the hot valley and got nowhere. Up in the mountains, there are dogwoods to remind me of other springs, with dogwoods in full glory.

✒ *My Favorite Christmas Present*

December 25th, I was invited out for the evening. In the morning, I was working on my slides when the phone rang. My first inclination was to ignore it. Then I remembered it was Christmas Day and answered it. It was my sister wishing me a Merry Christmas. While talking to her, I happened to look out and saw trees coated with ice, a rare occasion in California. After hanging up the phone, I grabbed my camera and dashed out. The ice crystals in the hairs of the stem were more beautiful than any decorations I put on the tree.

Thanks for calling, my dear sister.

Mimulus cardinalis

☙ Ancient Wisdom

An old Chinese saying warns about trusting books too much. If one believes completely what one reads, one is better off not reading. The book says Red Monkey Flowers bloom in August to October. We could not find a single one in September. I did see it the following June behind some blackberry and poison oak, and decided to walk through the blackberry as the lesser of the two evils.

Castilleja affinis

❧ *So Difficult*

It is easy to recognize an Indian Paintbrush, but difficult to key it down to species.
I am never sure.

94

95

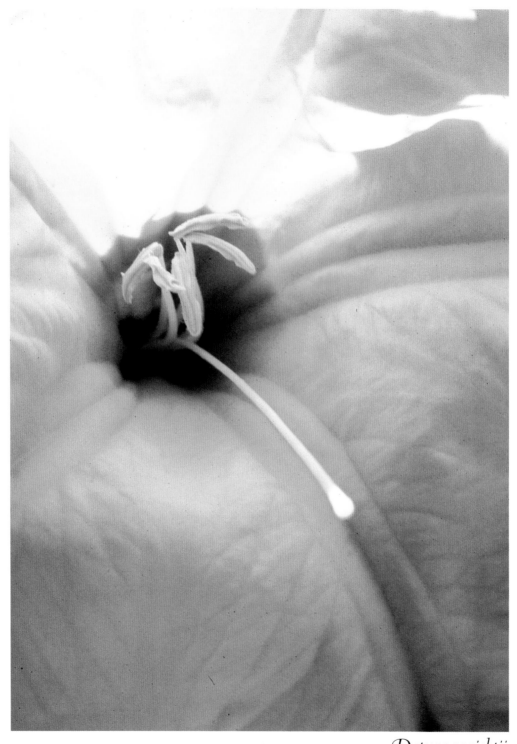

Datura wrightii

Datura wrightii

97

❧ *Wait Till You Meet Them*

Jimsonweed was one of the targets of our herbicide program, something we tried to eradicate. I had no feeling for it until I saw it in the desert. It has very interesting large trumpet flowers. When the bud unfurls, it goes through lovely forms and finally turns into a large white flower.

After that first encounter, I had misgivings about killing Jimsonweed. My colleagues had to reassure me that it was a pest for the farmers, poisonous to animals, and we could never wipe out Jimsonweed completely.

Nothing is clearly black and white.

Zantedeschia aethiopica
(native of S. Africa)

Oh! I (You) Missed It

We were at the Whalers Cove of Point Lobos State Reserve in front of an old cottage. The weathered wood with dark grain looked interesting and I took a picture of the planks. I thought it might be too plain and I included a bush of Calla Lily at the corner. The flowers were very eye-catching and very few people noticed the wood.

The flowers were at different stages, just opening, full bloom, and spent. Some people wished I had cut away the brown heads. Others thought the stages represented past, present, and future, and were wonderful. The truth was I did not pay much attention to the flowers, only the wood.

So often we have difficulty making others see what we want them to see. However, others can teach us to see what we miss.

Eschscholzia californica

❧ Poppies And Hostesses

In the spring of 1992, Lillian and I went to Lancaster to see wildflowers. On one county road, we saw two new houses with front yards full of weeds and poppies. We assumed they were not yet occupied, and stopped by the roadside to take pictures. Shortly afterward, a woman came out and told us to leave. We did.

Next spring, we were up in the Sonora area and could not resist some magnificent poppies in someone's garden. We gathered our courage and went in to ask permission to photograph the poppies. The hostess insisted we move our car into their driveway to be out of harm's way. She showed us around and told us other places of colors. She also invited us, two total strangers, to come back.

People are different.

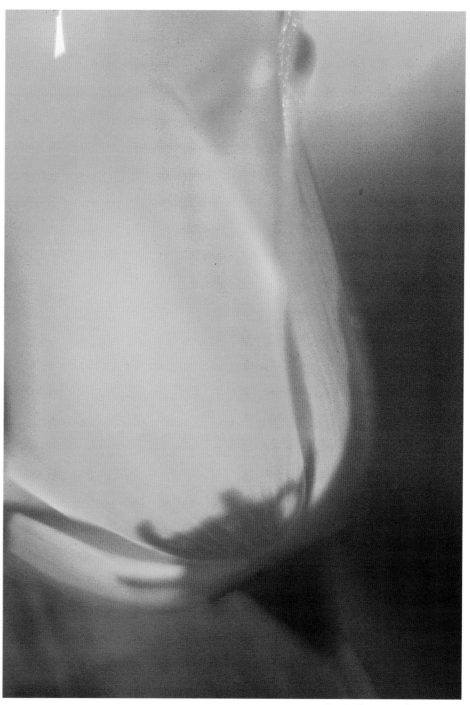

Eschscholzia californica

103

Eschscholzia californica

❧ *I Am A Sucker For. . .*

Early in 1998, I counted 162 slides of California Poppy in my files. Any person with any sense will agree that is enough. I promised myself not to take another poppy picture, except. . .

The highway to heaven is paved with golden poppies.

105

Everybody needs beauty as well as bread, places to play in and pray in, where nature may heal and cheer and give strength to body and soul.

John Muir, 1838–1914

Eschscholzia lemmonii

❧ Earth Notes

Once more wildflowers
Splash with color roadside, fields
And hills—as always.

    Only by walking:
    Dew on toes, star-flower glimpsed.
    Bird and worm's progress.

Lichen-colored rock
Is red, yellow-gray, moss-green:
Nature's peace symbol.

    Old earth, wrinkled, scarred,
    Has gifts for us, and wisdom.
    Our task is to learn.

Virginia K. Anderson, Times And Seasons, ©1985

Cuyama Valley

ᕦ For you shall go out in joy, and be led back in peace. The mountains and hills before you shall burst into song, and all the trees of the field shall clap their hands.

Isaiah 55:12

Bear Valley

The wilderness and the dry land shall be glad, the desert shall rejoice and blossom; like crocus it shall blossom abundantly, and rejoice with joy and singing. They shall see the glory of the Lord, and majesty of our God.

Isaiah 35:1-2

﹌ Can You Smell The Sea?

Grass on the sand dune at Point Reyes National Seashore, enough sea breezes to bend the blades so they caught the sunlight. Ice plant and daisy added colors. No, I could not see the ocean, but I could feel it. Some people asked me how could a scientist believe in God. It is easy, one can feel the presence of God.

❧ Thanks for the Encouragement

One time this picture was hung in Stone Hall at Trinity United Methodist Church in Berkeley. A friend's father, who is also a photographer, was visiting our church. He told me he liked this picture very much. He added that the subject was so ordinary, he would not have taken a picture if he came upon it; I had eyes for seeing. Thank you, Mr. Mills. A compliment works as encouragement; we all need it.

III

❧ When Life Gives You a Lemon

The rain came down harder and harder. The wind blew stronger and stronger. The group gave up and headed toward the cars. One last picture. . .

Every Storm Cloud has a Silver Lining

Our tenth wedding anniversary was coming up; I had picked out a gift he would like. Before I could get it, he told me he wanted to leave. I was too proud to beg him to stay and too stubborn to follow him, so we parted. It hurt! It was not too bad at work. As a matter of fact, in order to concentrate, I wrote research reports, which caught up with the experiments. But evenings and weekends seemed very long. With Thanksgiving, Christmas, and New Year holidays coming up, I knew it would be very difficult. To help me get through it, I booked a tour to Tahiti, New Zealand, Australia and Fiji. This was 1975; not many people visited there. My colleagues asked me to bring back lots of pictures, and I did not even own a camera!

All the time we were married, he always told me I had no artistic sense and I should not waste film in taking pictures. After the divorce, he took the camera. I consulted a few friends, bought a Rollei 35 camera, read the instructions, and tried a roll of film. It developed okay and off I went.

After the trip, I gave a slide show at work. Lillian Troxell liked it and asked me to go to the desert with her to see and photograph wildflowers. It took me three years to agree. The Rollei could not take close-up pictures and I was not sure I wanted to invest in a new camera, so I borrowed one. We spent a week in the Mojave Desert, and I was hooked. I have not stopped taking pictures.

If our marriage had worked, I probably never would have picked up a camera and missed all the fun. Life has strange twists and turns.

In late 1982, Ruby Harmon's husband passed away. She told me how she came to California during World War II, met Mr. Harmon and married him. One item struck me as unusual in all those years; she had never been to Yosemite. I promised to take her there, not in the winter, but in the spring of 1983. I asked Lillian Troxell to come along and we had a wonderful time. Ruby got to love wildflowers as much as we did. When we got back home, Ruby insisted I share the slides with our friends at church. In sharing, the pleasure multiplied.

With help and encouragement from many friends, these pictures are collected here in a book, so they can reach more people. I hope you enjoy them as much as I do.